Goose berry Patch co.®

101 *Christmas* RECIPES

Gooseberry Patch
2500 Farmers Dr., #110
Columbus, OH 43235

www.gooseberrypatch.com
1·800·854·6673

Gooseberry Patch *cookbooks*

Since 1992, we've been publishing our own country cookbooks for every kitchen and for every meal of the day! Each title has hundreds of budget-friendly recipes, using ingredients you already have on hand in your pantry.

In addition, you'll find helpful tips and ideas on every page, along with our hand-drawn artwork and plenty of personality. Their lay-flat binding makes them so easy to use...they're sure to become a fast favorite in your kitchen.

Call us toll-free at
1•800•854•6673
and we'd be delighted to tell you all about our newest titles!

Shop with us online anytime at
www.gooseberrypatch.com

Send us your favorite recipe!

*and the memory that makes it special for you!** If we select your recipe for a brand-new **Gooseberry Patch** cookbook, your name will appear right along with it...and you'll receive a FREE copy of the book!

Submit your recipe on our website at
www.gooseberrypatch.com

Or mail to:

Gooseberry Patch • Attn: Cookbook Dept.
2500 Farmers Dr., #110 • Columbus, OH 43235

*Please include the number of servings and all other necessary information!

Have a taste for more?

Visit **www.gooseberrypatch.com**
to join our **Circle of Friends**!

- Free recipes, tips and ideas plus a complete cookbook index
- Get special email offers and our monthly E-letter delivered to your inbox
- Find local stores with **Gooseberry Patch** cookbooks, calendars and organizers

CONTENTS

Dedication

To everyone who believes that the best part of the holidays is enjoying favorite foods with family & friends!

Appreciation

Warmest thanks to all of our friends who shared their tastiest, most festive recipes with us!

Jalapeño Cheese Spread

2 8-oz. pkgs. cream cheese,
    softened
1 t. lemon juice
3 to 4 roasted jalapeño peppers,
    seeded and chopped
2-oz. jar diced pimentos,
    drained
1 T. mayonnaise
1/8 t. salt
assorted crackers or tortillas

Combine all ingredients except
crackers or tortillas. Mix well. Cover
and refrigerate overnight. Serve with
crackers or spread on warmed
tortillas. Makes about 2 cups.

7

Kerri Cordova
Martinez, CA
My grandmother used to make
this spread every
Christmas...with red and
green colors, it's perfect
for the holidays!

Greek Spread

Stephanie Doyle
Lincoln University, PA

A must for festive parties...my guests always request it!

1 c. plus 1 T. chopped almonds, divided
8-oz. pkg. crumbled feta cheese
7-oz. jar roasted red peppers, drained and chopped
1 clove garlic, chopped
2 8-oz. pkgs. cream cheese, softened
10-oz. pkg. frozen spinach, thawed and drained
assorted crackers or toasted pita wedges

Line a 2-quart bowl with plastic wrap; sprinkle in one tablespoon almonds. In a separate large bowl, mix together 1/2 cup almonds, feta cheese, peppers, garlic, cream cheese and spinach; blend well. Press into bowl over almonds. Cover and chill overnight. At serving time, invert onto a serving dish. Remove plastic wrap; press remaining almonds onto the outside. Serve with crackers or pita wedges. Makes about 7 cups.

Seafood Pinwheels

8-oz. pkg. cream cheese, softened
8-oz. pkg. imitation crabmeat, shredded
1/2 c. red pepper, chopped
1/2 c. shredded Cheddar cheese
2 green onions, chopped
1/4 c. fresh parsley, chopped
1/2 to 1 t. hot pepper sauce
chili powder to taste
6 6-inch flour tortillas
Garnish: paprika

Beat cream cheese until smooth; stir in crabmeat, red pepper, shredded cheese, onions, parsley and sauce. Sprinkle with chili powder; stir until well blended. Spread cheese mixture evenly over tortillas; roll up tightly. Slice off ends; wrap in plastic wrap. Refrigerate for 2 hours to overnight. When ready to serve, slice each roll into 6 slices. Arrange on a baking sheet sprayed with non-stick vegetable spray. Bake at 350 degrees for 10 to 12 minutes, until bubbly. Sprinkle with paprika; serve warm. Makes about 3 dozen.

Wendy Lee Paffenroth
Pine Island, NY

I like to top each pinwheel with a little slice of Muenster cheese, then broil for 30 seconds until the cheese is golden.

Spiced Christmas Cashews

1 egg white
1 T. water
2 9-3/4 oz. cans salted cashews
1/3 c. sugar
1 T. chili powder
2 t. salt
2 t. ground cumin
1/2 t. cayenne pepper

Whisk together egg white and water in a large bowl. Add cashews; toss to coat. Transfer to a colander; drain for 2 minutes. In a separate bowl, combine sugar and spices; add cashews and toss to coat. Arrange in a single layer on a greased 15"x10" jelly-roll pan. Bake at 250 degrees for 50 to 55 minutes, stirring once. Cool on a wire rack. Store in an airtight container. Makes about 3-1/2 cups.

Paula Marchesi
Lenhartsville, PA

Sweet, salty, crunchy and oh-so snackable! Everybody raves about them. I often make 10 to 12 batches for holiday gifts...maybe more!

Peppermint Punch

1 qt. peppermint ice cream,
　softened
1 c. milk
2-ltr. bottle ginger ale, chilled
Garnish: peppermint sticks,
　finely crushed or whole

In a large punch bowl, blend together
ice cream and milk; stir gently. Slowly
add ginger ale; stir until combined.
Moisten rims of glasses with water
and dip into finely crushed candy.
Serve with peppermint stick stirrers,
if desired. Serves 8 to 10.

Christi Ross
Grundy Center, IA

My husband's grandmother's
recipe. A former restaurant
owner, Grandma Ross was
known far and wide for this
festive and tasty punch.

Smoked Salmon Dip

8-oz. container cream cheese,
   softened
2 T. fresh dill, chopped
1 T. lemon juice
4-oz. pkg. smoked salmon,
   chopped and divided
Optional: fresh dill sprigs
assorted crackers

Combine first 3 ingredients in a food
processor. Add half of salmon; process
until smooth. Fold in remaining half
of salmon. Garnish with dill sprigs,
if desired. Serve with crackers. Makes
10 to 12 servings.

Jo Ann
Gooseberry Patch

We love to enjoy
this luscious dip with
sesame bread sticks.

Gingered Coconut Chicken Fingers

Rogene Rogers
Bemidji, MN
These are always a hit
at get-togethers!

3/4 c. sweetened flaked coconut
3 T. plain dry bread crumbs
3/4 t. ground ginger
1/2 t. cayenne pepper
2 T. honey
1 t. lemon or orange juice
14-oz. pkg. chicken tenders,
    sliced in half crosswise
salt to taste

In a blender or food processor, combine coconut, bread crumbs and spices. Pulse to blend; transfer to a shallow dish. Blend honey and juice in a separate shallow dish. Sprinkle chicken pieces with salt; coat in honey mixture and roll in coconut mixture. Place on a baking sheet that has been sprayed with non-stick vegetable spray. Bake at 400 degrees for 12 to 15 minutes, until chicken is tender and no longer pink. Serve with Sour Cream Sauce. Makes about one dozen.

Sour Cream Sauce:

1/3 c. sour cream
2 T. crushed pineapple with juice
1/4 t. ground ginger

Mix well; chill until serving time.

13

Nachos for a Crowd

13-1/2 oz. bag round tortilla chips
15-oz. can homestyle chili
8-oz. pkg. shredded Mexican-
  blend cheese
1/2 c. queso sauce
10-oz. pkg. shredded lettuce
1 onion, diced
1 green pepper, chopped
1/2 c. jalapeño pepper, sliced
Optional: 1/2 c. sliced black olives,
  4-oz. can diced green chiles
Garnish: 1/2 c. sour cream,
  1 tomato, diced, 2 T. dried
  chives

Arrange chips on a large microwave-safe plate; set aside. Heat chili in a microwave-safe bowl on high setting for one minute; stir. Microwave for another minute; set aside. Sprinkle tortilla chips with cheese; microwave on high setting for 30 seconds. Spoon chili and queso sauce over cheese; sprinkle with lettuce, onion and peppers. Top with black olives and green chiles, if desired. Add a dollop of sour cream; sprinkle with tomato and chives. Serves 6 to 8.

Colleen Seaton
Nashville, TN

A real party starter!
If you like, substitute
1-1/2 cups of your own
homemade chili.

Brie with Caramelized Onions

5-oz. wheel Brie cheese
1 onion, chopped
2 T. butter
1/2 c. brown sugar, packed
1/2 c. sweetened dried
    cranberries
2 T. balsamic vinegar
1/4 c. pistachio nuts, chopped
assorted crackers

Slice top off cheese. Place cheese in a greased 9" pie plate; bake at 350 degrees for 10 minutes. Remove from oven; set aside. In a saucepan over medium heat, sauté onion in butter until tender, about 5 minutes. Add brown sugar, berries and vinegar. Cook until mixture caramelizes and thickens, about 5 minutes. Spoon mixture over cheese; sprinkle with pistachios. Serve warm with crackers. Serves 6.

Kathleen Richter Niedbala
Bridgeport, CT

This is a hit at any holiday gathering. Serve with baguette slices for a very simple yet elegant appetizer.

Garlic-Romano Dipping Sauce

1 c. grated Romano cheese
1/4 t. red pepper flakes
1/2 c. olive oil
1 clove garlic, pressed
1 loaf Italian bread, cubed

Whisk together all ingredients except bread in a small bowl; mix until well combined. Cover and refrigerate until ready to serve. Bring sauce to room temperature before serving with bread. Makes 1-1/2 cups.

Denise Mainville
Huber Heights, OH

This sauce is also delicious drizzled over steamed vegetables.

Glazed Kielbasa Bites

1 lb. Kielbasa, sliced
1 c. apricot preserves
1/2 c. maple syrup
2 T. bourbon or apple juice

Combine all ingredients in a slow cooker. Cover and cook on low setting for 4 hours. Serves 8 to 10.

17

Janice Dorsey
San Antonio, TX

Everybody loves these savory morsels of sausage from the slow cooker!

Tomato & Basil Tartlets

Rogene Rogers
Bemidji, MN

These tasty tarts
are always welcome on
a brunch buffet.

1-2/3 c. all-purpose flour
1/4 t. salt
1/2 c. butter-flavored shortening
2 to 3 T. ice water
2 eggs, beaten
3 T. whipping cream
3 T. crumbled feta cheese
salt and pepper to taste
1/2 lb. roma tomatoes, chopped
12 fresh basil leaves, cut in thin
 ribbons

Combine flour and salt in a medium bowl. Cut in shortening with a pastry blender until mixture resembles coarse crumbs. Sprinkle in water, one tablespoon at a time, tossing lightly with a fork until dough forms a ball. On a lightly floured surface, roll out dough about 1/8-inch thick. Cut out 18 rounds with a fluted 2-1/2" round cookie cutter. Press gently into ungreased mini muffin cups. Whisk eggs and cream in a separate bowl. Stir in cheese, salt and pepper; set aside. In a small saucepan over low heat, warm tomatoes with basil. Drain well; stir into egg mixture. Spoon evenly into tartlets. Bake for 10 minutes at 400 degrees. Reduce oven to 350 degrees; bake until filling sets and pastry is golden, about 10 minutes. Cool on a wire rack. Makes 18.

Cranberry & Blue Cheese Ball

8-oz. pkg. cream cheese, softened

1 c. sharp white Cheddar cheese, shredded

4-oz. container crumbled blue cheese

6-oz. pkg. sweetened dried cranberries

assorted crackers

Place all ingredients except crackers into a food processor; process until well combined. Shape cheese mixture into a ball on a length of plastic wrap; wrap well and refrigerate overnight. Let stand at room temperature for 30 minutes before serving. Serve with assorted crackers. Makes about 3 cups.

19

Kristie Rigo
Friedens, PA

This yummy, super-easy cheese ball is perfect for the holidays.

Mrs. Claus' Christmas Bread

1 c. sugar
2 T. butter, softened
1 egg, beaten
2 c. all-purpose flour
1 t. baking powder
1/2 t. baking soda
1/2 t. salt
3/4 c. orange juice
1 c. cranberries, chopped
1/2 c. chopped pecans

Blend sugar, butter and egg together in a large bowl. Add remaining ingredients; mix well and pour into a greased 9"x5" loaf pan. Bake at 350 degrees for 45 to 50 minutes. Makes one loaf.

Francie Stutzman
Dalton, Ohio
Packed with delicious fruit and nuts...share a loaf with a friend!

Chocolate Eggnog

2 qts. eggnog
16-oz. can chocolate syrup
Optional: 1/2 c. light rum
1 c. whipping cream
2 T. powdered sugar
Garnish: baking cocoa

Combine eggnog, chocolate syrup and rum, if using, in a punch bowl, stirring well. Beat whipping cream with an electric mixer on high speed until foamy. Add powdered sugar; continue beating until stiff peaks form. Dollop whipped cream over eggnog; sift cocoa over top. Serve immediately. Makes 3 quarts.

Valarie Dennard
Palatka, FL
A great no-fuss recipe for jazzing up store-bought eggnog.

Zesty Brunch Quiche

1 c. shredded Cheddar cheese
4 slices bacon, crisply cooked
  and crumbled
2 green onions, thinly sliced
9-inch frozen pie crust
3 eggs, beaten
1/2 c. milk
1/2 c. salsa

Sprinkle cheese, bacon and onions into
pie crust; set aside. Whisk eggs, milk
and salsa together; pour into pie crust.
Carefully place on a baking sheet; bake
at 375 degrees for 35 minutes. Let
stand 10 minutes before slicing.
Serves 6.

Patty Schroyer
Baxter, IA

Try using peach or apricot
salsa for a whole
new taste.

Chocolate-Cherry Cream Scones

2 c. all-purpose flour
1 T. baking powder
1/2 t. salt
1/4 c. sugar
1/4 c. mini semi-sweet
   chocolate chips
1/2 c. dried cherries, chopped
1-1/4 c. whipping cream
Garnish: additional cream,
   coarse sugar

Combine flour, baking powder, salt and sugar in a bowl; whisk to blend well. Add chocolate chips and cherries. Stir dry ingredients while pouring in cream, continuing to stir until a soft, sticky dough is formed. Turn out onto a lightly floured surface and knead 8 to 10 times. Pat dough into a circle 1/2-inch to 3/4-inch thick; cut into 8 wedges. Place wedges one inch apart on a parchment paper-lined baking sheet. Brush with cream; sprinkle generously with coarse sugar. Bake at 425 degrees until golden and springy to the touch, about 15 minutes. Makes 8.

23

Michelle Stewart
West Richland, WA

This recipe was passed on to me by a dear friend. These scones are absolutely irresistible, especially warm from the oven!

Jumbo Cinnamon Rolls

1 c. very warm milk (110 degrees)
1 env. active dry yeast
1/2 c. sugar
2 eggs, beaten
1/3 c. margarine, melted and cooled
1 t. salt
4-1/2 c. all-purpose flour
3/4 c. brown sugar, packed
1/3 c. butter, softened
2-1/2 T. cinnamon
16-oz. container cream cheese
   frosting

Combine milk, yeast and sugar in a large bowl; let stand for 10 minutes. Stir in eggs and margarine with a wooden spoon. Mix salt into flour; add flour to wet mixture one cup at a time until dough forms. Knead until smooth; place dough in a large bowl sprayed with non-stick vegetable spray. Cover; let rest until double in size. Generously spray a surface with non-stick vegetable spray; roll out dough into a 21-inch by 16-inch rectangle. Spread with butter; combine brown sugar and cinnamon and sprinkle over top. Roll up dough and slice into 12 rolls; arrange in a lightly greased 13"x9" baking pan. Cover and let rise until nearly double in size, about 30 minutes. Bake at 400 degrees until golden, about 15 minutes. Spread warm rolls with frosting; serve warm. Makes one dozen.

Carol Courter
Delaware, OH

Mmm...treat the whole family to these scrumptious, ooey-gooey warm rolls!

Farmers' Breakfast Casserole

3 c. frozen shredded hashbrowns
1 c. shredded Cheddar or
    Monterey Jack cheese
1 c. cooked ham or bacon, diced
1/4 c. green onion, diced
4 eggs, beaten
12-oz. can evaporated milk
1/4 t. pepper
1/8 t. salt

Arrange hashbrowns evenly in the bottom of a greased 13"x9" baking pan. Sprinkle with cheese, ham or bacon and onion; set aside. Combine eggs, milk, pepper and salt in a medium bowl; blend well. Pour egg mixture over hashbrown mixture; cover and refrigerate for several hours to overnight. Bake, uncovered, at 350 degrees until center is set, 40 to 45 minutes. If chilled overnight, bake for 55 to 60 minutes. Makes 6 to 8 servings.

25

Laurie Anderson
Columbia, TN
A complete, extra-hearty breakfast...simply add fresh fruit and a warm beverage.

Old-Fashioned Blueberry Pancakes

2 c. milk
2 eggs, beaten
1/2 c. sour cream
2 c. all-purpose flour
2 T. baking powder
2 T. sugar
1/2 t. salt
1/4 c. oil
1 c. blueberries

Combine milk, eggs and sour cream;
beat well. Stir together flour, baking
powder, sugar and salt; add to milk
mixture. Beat until lumps disappear;
mix in oil. Fold in blueberries; pour
1/4 cup batter per pancake onto a
greased hot griddle. Flip when bubbles
appear. Serves 4 to 6.

Sharon Sorrels
Troutville, VA

An all-time favorite...try
topping pancakes with
blueberry syrup for a
very, berry flavor!

Malted Hot Cocoa

6 1-oz. sqs. bittersweet baking
   chocolate, chopped
1/2 c. boiling water
1/2 c. whipping cream
1 c. milk
3 T. malted milk powder
Garnish: whipped topping,
   crushed malted milk ball
   candies

Place chocolate in a small bowl;
pour boiling water over chocolate.
Let stand for 3 minutes. In a small
saucepan, combine cream and milk
over medium heat; bring to a
simmer. Stir in malted milk powder;
set aside. Whisk chocolate mixture
until smooth; add to milk mixture.
Garnish with whipped topping and
crushed candies. Serves 4.

27

JoAnna Brown
Ann Arbor, MI

A hot, creamy beverage
that's just a little
different.

Heat & Hold Scrambled Eggs

1 doz. eggs, beaten
1-1/3 c. milk
1 t. salt
1/8 t. pepper
2 T. all-purpose flour
1 T. pimento, chopped
1 T. fresh parsley, chopped
1/4 c. butter

Combine all ingredients except butter in a large bowl. Whisk until smooth and set aside. Melt butter in a large skillet over low heat; pour egg mixture into skillet. Cook and stir until eggs are set to desired consistency. Can be held for up to one hour in a chafing dish or an electric skillet set at 200 degrees. Serves 6.

Judy Collins
Nashville, TN
Serve with a stack of buttered toast and a platter of sizzling sausage links...yum!

Emma's Gingerbread Muffins

1 c. sugar
1/2 c. margarine, softened
1/2 c. shortening
3 eggs
1/2 c. molasses
1/2 c. golden or light corn syrup
3 c. all-purpose flour
2 t. cinnamon
2 t. ground ginger
1 t. nutmeg
1-3/4 t. baking soda
1 c. buttermilk

Blend together sugar, margarine and shortening. Beat in eggs, one at a time. Add molasses and corn syrup; set aside. Sift together flour and spices. Dissolve baking soda in buttermilk; add to batter alternately with flour. Fill greased and floured muffin cups 2/3 full. Bake at 350 degrees for about 15 minutes. Makes 2 dozen.

29

Bernadette Dobias
Houston, TX
These muffins are moist, spicy and delicious. I received this recipe from a friend's mother.

Nutty Maple Waffles

1-1/2 c. all-purpose flour
2 T. sugar
1 t. baking powder
1/4 t. salt
2 eggs, separated
12-oz. can evaporated milk
3 T. oil
1/2 t. maple extract
1/2 c. pecans, finely chopped

Combine flour, sugar, baking powder and salt in a medium bowl; mix well and set aside. Combine egg yolks, evaporated milk, oil and extract in a large bowl; blend well. Gradually add flour mixture, beating well after each addition; set aside. In a small bowl, beat egg whites with an electric mixer on high until stiff peaks form; fold into batter. For each waffle, pour 1/2 cup batter onto a preheated, greased waffle iron; sprinkle with one tablespoon nuts. Bake according to manufacturer's instructions. Makes 8 servings.

Vickie
Gooseberry Patch

Crunchy pecans paired with maple...a great way to begin the day! Top with plenty of butter and rich maple syrup.

Eggnog French Toast Strata

Sandy Bogan
Waldorf, MD
A convenient overnight
make-ahead for breakfast.

1 loaf French bread, sliced
3-oz. pkg. cream cheese,
   softened
2-1/2 c. eggnog
6 T. butter, melted
8 eggs, beaten
1/4 t. nutmeg

Arrange enough bread slices to cover
the bottom of a greased 13"x9" baking
pan. Spread cream cheese over bread;
arrange remaining bread over top.
Whisk together eggnog, butter and
eggs until blended. Pour evenly
over bread. With back of spoon,
gently press bread into dish. Sprinkle
with nutmeg. Cover and refrigerate
for 8 hours to overnight. Uncover;
bake at 325 degrees for 30 to
35 minutes, until center is set
and edges are golden. Let stand for
10 minutes; cut into squares. Serve
with warm Cranberry Syrup. Makes
6 to 8 servings.

Cranberry Syrup:

1 c. frozen raspberry juice
   concentrate, thawed
1 c. whole-berry cranberry sauce
1/3 c. sugar

Combine in a saucepan over low
heat. Cook and whisk until bubbly.

31

Christmas Eve Soup

2 c. potatoes, peeled and diced
1/2 c. carrot, peeled and diced
1/2 c. celery, chopped
1/4 c. onion, chopped
2 c. water
1-1/2 t. salt
1/4 t. pepper
1 c. cooked ham, cubed
1/4 c. margarine
1/4 c. all-purpose flour
2 c. milk
8-oz. pkg. shredded
   Cheddar cheese

Combine vegetables, water, salt and pepper in a large soup pot. Bring to a boil over medium heat. Reduce heat; cover and simmer until vegetables are tender. Stir in ham; set aside. In a separate saucepan, melt margarine; stir in flour until smooth. Gradually add milk; bring to a boil. Cook and stir for 2 minutes, until thickened. Stir in cheese until melted; add to vegetable mixture and heat through. Serves 8.

Jessica Heimbaugh
Gilbert, IA
My mom and I wanted to share one of our favorite recipes. We always have this soup on Christmas Eve...we hope you'll enjoy it too!

Ham & Swiss Cheese Rolls

3/4 c. margarine
1-1/2 T. Worcestershire sauce
1/2 t. dry mustard
1-1/2 t. poppy seed
2 t. dried, minced onion
2 12-ct. pkgs. Hawaiian rolls
1 lb. thinly sliced deli ham
1/2 lb. sliced Swiss cheese

Combine margarine, Worcestershire sauce, mustard, poppy seed and onion in a small saucepan. Bring to a boil over medium heat; remove from heat. Slice individual rolls in half. Make sandwiches using bread, ham and cheese. Place sandwiches on an ungreased 15"x10" jelly-roll pan. Spoon margarine mixture over sandwiches. Bake, uncovered, at 350 degrees for 15 minutes. Makes 12 servings.

33

Janet Stewart
Owensboro, KY
This recipe is a favorite at our Mothers of Preschoolers (MOPS) church group.

Cheddar Potato Gratin

2 t. dried sage
1-1/2 t. salt
1/2 t. pepper
3 lbs. potatoes, peeled, thinly
  sliced and divided
1 onion, thinly sliced and divided
8-oz. pkg. shredded Cheddar
  cheese, divided
1 c. whipping cream
1 c. chicken broth

Mix sage, salt and pepper in a cup; set aside. Layer 1/3 of potatoes and half of onion in a lightly greased 13"x9" baking pan. Sprinkle with one teaspoon of sage mixture and 1/3 of cheese. Repeat layers with remaining ingredients, ending with cheese. Whisk cream and broth together until well blended; pour evenly over top. Bake, covered, at 400 degrees for one hour, until tender and golden. Let stand 5 minutes before serving. Makes 10 to 12 servings.

Jo Ann
Gooseberry Patch
Everyone's favorite cheesy potatoes...especially scrumptious with baked ham.

Mexican Albondigas Soup

2 lbs. lean ground beef
1 c. Italian-seasoned dry bread
   crumbs
1 egg, beaten
Optional: 1/4 c. olive oil
3 stalks celery, sliced
1 green pepper, diced
1 c. carrots, peeled and diced
15-1/4 oz. can corn, drained
2 14-oz. cans beef broth
10-oz. can diced tomatoes with
   chiles
4-oz. can diced green chiles
3 c. cooked rice
2 T. fresh cilantro, finely chopped
2 T. onion, minced
1 t. garlic powder
1 t. ground cumin
1 t. chili powder
1 t. salt
1/2 t. pepper
4 to 5 c. water

Combine ground beef, bread crumbs
and egg; form into one-inch balls.
Brown in a skillet over medium heat,
adding oil if desired; drain. Place
meatballs in a slow cooker and set
aside. In a small saucepan, cover celery,
green pepper and carrots with a little
water. Cook until tender; add to slow
cooker with remaining ingredients.
Cover and cook on low setting for
3 to 4 hours. Serves 8.

Sherry Sheehan
Phoenix, AZ

My Hispanic pastor tells
me this tasty slow-cooker
soup tastes just like
the soup his mother
used to make.

Marie's Vegetable Soup

3 to 3-1/2 lb. beef chuck roast
1 head cabbage, quartered
2 onions, chopped
46-oz. can tomato juice
4 15-oz. cans mixed vegetables
28-oz. can diced tomatoes
6-oz. can tomato paste
salt and pepper to taste
Optional: hot pepper sauce to taste

Place roast in an ungreased large roasting pan; cover. Bake at 325 degrees for 1-1/2 hours, until half done. Add cabbage and onions to pan; add enough water to cover. Bake an additional one to 1-1/2 hours, until roast is very tender. Transfer contents of roasting pan to a large soup pot; stir in remaining ingredients except hot sauce. Simmer over medium-low heat for one to 1-1/2 hours. At serving time, break up any large pieces of roast; add pepper sauce, if desired. Makes about 10 servings.

Marie Needham
Columbus, OH

My mother gave me this hearty recipe many years ago. The "secret ingredient" is the cabbage!

Pizzawiches

1 lb. ground beef
1 onion, diced
4-oz. jar sliced mushrooms,
    drained
16-oz. jar pizza sauce
6 to 8 slices mozzarella cheese
6 to 8 hamburger or sub buns,
    split
Optional: sliced olives,
    pepperoni slices

37

In a skillet over medium heat, brown ground beef and onion; drain. Add mushrooms and pizza sauce to skillet; heat through. Assemble sandwiches with ground beef mixture and cheese slices, adding olives and pepperoni if desired. Serves 6 to 8.

Jessica Robertson
Fishers, IN
A tasty twist on good ol'
Sloppy Joes...kids love
these sandwiches!

Twice-Baked Sweet Potatoes

6 sweet potatoes
1/2 c. plus 1 T. butter, melted
  and divided
6 T. apple juice
2 T. brown sugar, packed
1/2 t. ground ginger
1 c. mini marshmallows
1/3 c. sweetened flaked coconut

Bake sweet potatoes at 375 degrees for
50 to 60 minutes, until tender. Cool
slightly. Partially slice potatoes
lengthwise; scoop out centers, leaving
1/8-inch thick shells. Mash potato pulp
in a medium bowl. Add 1/2 cup butter,
apple juice, brown sugar and ginger;
beat until fluffy. Spoon into shells.
Mix together marshmallows, coconut
and remaining butter; spoon over
potatoes. Bake at 350 degrees for
20 to 25 minutes, until heated
through. Makes 6 servings.

Tiffini Lyons
Naples, FL

A delicious variation on
the traditional sweet
potato casserole.

Herbed Corn Bake

1/4 c. butter
1/2 c. cream cheese, softened
1/4 t. onion salt
1 T. fresh chives, chopped
10-oz. pkg. frozen corn, thawed

Melt butter in a heavy saucepan over low heat. Add cream cheese, onion salt and chives, stirring until cheese melts. Add corn; mix well. Spoon into an ungreased 1-1/2 quart casserole dish. Cover and bake at 325 degrees until bubbly, about 45 minutes. Makes 4 servings.

39

Nikole Morningstar
Norfolk, VA

This dish always reminds me of my mom...she loved creating new dishes for our family to enjoy.

Snow Fun
Creamy Tuna Melts

2 to 3 stalks celery, diced
1 onion, diced
12-oz. can tuna, drained
1/2 c. cottage cheese
1/2 c. mayonnaise
1/4 t. garlic salt
1/8 t. sugar
4 English muffins, split and
   toasted
8 slices American cheese

In a skillet sprayed with non-stick
cooking spray, sauté celery and onion
until tender. Add tuna, cottage cheese,
mayonnaise, garlic salt and sugar to
skillet. Mix well, breaking up tuna.
Cook over low heat until warmed
through, stirring frequently; remove
from heat. Place toasted muffins
cut-side up on a broiler pan. Spread
with tuna mixture; top with cheese
slices. Broil until cheese melts; serve
immediately. Makes 8 servings.

Cindy Atkins
Vancouver, WA
Oh-so warm and cozy after
an afternoon of sledding
or skating!

Cape Cod Clam Chowder

2 10-3/4 oz. cans New England
   clam chowder
10-3/4 oz. can cream of
   celery soup
10-3/4 oz. can cream of
   potato soup
2 pts. half-and-half
3 potatoes, peeled and diced
salt and pepper to taste
Optional: chopped fresh chives

Combine soups and half-and-half
in a large stockpot. Place over
medium-low heat until heated
through, stirring often. Set aside
over low heat. Boil potatoes in water
for about 10 minutes; drain and add
to soup mixture. Cook over medium
heat until potatoes are tender. Add
salt and pepper to taste. Garnish with
chives, if desired. Serves 6 to 8.

41

Robin Cornett
Spring Hill, FL
For smoky flavor, stir in
some crisply cooked and
crumbled bacon.

Ham & Cauliflower Au Gratin

2 10-oz. pkgs. frozen cauliflower, thawed and drained
1-1/4 c. smoked ham, chopped
10-3/4 oz. can Cheddar cheese soup
1/4 c. milk
2/3 c. biscuit baking mix
2 to 3 T. butter, softened
1/2 t. nutmeg
Garnish: dried parsley, paprika

Arrange cauliflower in an ungreased 13"x9" baking dish. Sprinkle with ham. Whisk together soup and milk until smooth; pour over top. Toss together biscuit mix, butter and nutmeg until crumbly; sprinkle over soup mixture. Sprinkle with parsley and paprika. Bake, uncovered, at 400 degrees until cauliflower is tender and topping is golden, 20 to 25 minutes. Makes 6 to 8 servings.

Tiffany Moore
Central Point, OR
One of my favorite recipes, because I know that my kids will eat their veggies without complaining!

Honeyed Carrots

5 c. carrots, peeled and sliced
1/4 c. honey
1/4 c. butter, melted
2 T. brown sugar, packed
2 T. fresh parsley, chopped
1/4 t. salt
1/8 t. pepper

Place carrots in a medium saucepan; add water to cover. Cook over medium heat just until tender; drain and set aside. Combine remaining ingredients in a small bowl and blend well. Pour honey mixture over carrots; toss to coat. Cook over medium heat until carrots are glazed and heated through. Makes 8 servings.

43

Jody Sinkula
Dresser, WI
The sweet taste of these carrots makes this a very popular dish!

Herb & Cheese Orzo

10-1/2 oz. can chicken broth
1 T. butter
1 c. orzo pasta, uncooked
1/2 c. shredded asiago cheese
1/8 c. fresh chives, minced
1/4 c. pine nuts, toasted

In a saucepan over medium heat, bring broth to a boil. Add butter and orzo; reduce heat and simmer until orzo absorbs broth, about 15 to 20 minutes. Stir in cheese, chives and pine nuts just before serving. Makes 4 servings.

Linda Karner
Pisgah Forest, NC

Creamy and delicious...a great side dish for roast chicken or pork.

Chili with Corn Dumplings

1-1/2 lbs. ground beef
3/4 c. onion, chopped
15-oz. can corn, divided
16-oz. can stewed tomatoes
16-oz. can tomato sauce
1 t. hot pepper sauce
2 T. chili powder
1 t. garlic, minced
1-1/3 c. biscuit baking mix
2/3 c. cornmeal
2/3 c. milk
3 T. fresh cilantro, chopped

Brown ground beef and onion in a Dutch oven over medium heat; drain. Set aside 1/2 cup corn; stir remaining corn with liquid, tomatoes, sauces, chili powder and garlic into beef mixture. Heat to boiling. Reduce heat; cover and simmer for 15 minutes. Mix baking mix and cornmeal in a medium bowl; stir in milk, cilantro and reserved corn just until moistened. Drop dough by rounded tablespoonfuls onto simmering chili. Cook over low heat, uncovered, for 15 minutes. Cover and cook an additional 15 to 18 minutes, until dumplings are dry on top. Serves 6.

45

Tanya Graham
Lawrenceville, GA
So simple, yet so satisfying on a chilly night.

Tomato Bisque

2 c. chicken broth
14-1/2 oz. can whole tomatoes,
  broken up
1/2 c. celery, chopped
1/2 c. onion, chopped
3 tomatoes, chopped
3 T. butter
3 T. all-purpose flour
2 c. half-and-half
1 T. sugar

In a large saucepan over medium heat,
combine broth, canned tomatoes,
celery and onion; bring to a boil.
Reduce heat; cover and simmer for
20 minutes. In a blender or food
processor, process mixture in small
batches until smooth. In the same
saucepan, cook chopped tomatoes in
butter for about 5 minutes; stir in
flour. Add half-and-half; cook and stir
over low heat until thickened. Stir in
processed broth mixture and sugar;
heat through without boiling. Makes
6 servings.

Sandy Spayer
Jeromesville, OH
An old-fashioned favorite,
perfect with a grilled
cheese sandwich.

Zesty Italian Beef

3-lb. beef chuck roast, quartered
1 to 2 T. oil
2-oz. pkg. zesty Italian salad
    dressing mix
12-oz. can beer or non-alcoholic
    beer
1 onion, chopped
6 to 7 pepperoncini peppers,
    chopped
6 to 8 sandwich buns, split

47

Brown roast in oil in a skillet over
medium heat; place into a slow
cooker. Sprinkle with dressing
mix; pour beer over top. Add
onion and peppers. Cover and cook
on high setting for 5 to 6 hours,
until meat shreds easily with a fork.
Spoon onto sandwich buns. Makes
6 to 8 sandwiches.

Jennifer Maxey
Mount Vernon, IL
The tender slow-cooker beef
will shred so easily that
sandwiches are a breeze
to make!

Rosemary-Garlic Skillet Potatoes

2 to 4 T. olive oil
2 T. butter
1-1/2 lbs. new redskin potatoes,
    sliced 1-inch thick
4 to 5 cloves garlic, minced
2-1/2 t. dried rosemary
1/2 t. salt
1/4 t. pepper

Add enough oil to a cast-iron skillet to completely cover bottom; add butter. Melt butter over medium heat and stir to mix with oil. Add potatoes and remaining ingredients. Mix well so that potatoes are throughly coated with oil mixture. Cook over medium heat for about 10 minutes, until potatoes are lightly golden. Transfer skillet to oven. Bake, uncovered, at 350 degrees for 30 minutes, or until potatoes are tender. Serves 4.

Jennifer Niemi
Nova Scotia, Canada
Crisp and golden...such a delicious way to enjoy tiny, fresh new potatoes.

Tena's Delicious Gumbo

4 14-1/2 oz. cans chicken broth
7-oz. pkg. gumbo mix with rice
5 to 6 boneless, skinless chicken
   breasts, cooked and chopped
1 lb. Polish sausage, cut into
   bite-size pieces
2 10-oz. pkgs. frozen chopped
   okra
1 green pepper, chopped
1 red pepper, chopped
1 onion, chopped
pepper to taste
Cajun seasoning to taste
2 14-oz. pkgs. frozen popcorn
   shrimp

Combine all ingredients except
shrimp in a large stockpot. Bring to
a boil; reduce heat, cover and simmer
for 25 minutes. Add shrimp; simmer
an additional 5 to 10 minutes. Serves
10 to 12.

49

Tena Hammond Graham
Evans, GA

This is so easy and
delicious! If you prefer,
substitute the broth the
chicken was simmered in.

Wisconsin Cheese Soup

5 T. butter
2 stalks celery, chopped
1/2 green pepper, chopped
5 mushrooms, chopped
2 carrots, chopped
1 onion, chopped
1/2 c. cooked ham, diced
1/2 c. all-purpose flour
2 T. cornstarch
4 c. chicken broth
4 c. milk
1/2 t. paprika
1/2 t. mustard
16-oz. pkg. shredded sharp
   Cheddar cheese
1/4 to 1/2 t. cayenne pepper
salt and pepper to taste

Melt butter in a stockpot over
medium heat; add vegetables and
ham. Cook until vegetables are tender,
about 10 minutes; stir in flour and
cornstarch. Cook for 3 minutes; add
broth and stir until thickened. Mix
in remaining ingredients; cook
until cheese is melted. Makes 8 to
10 servings.

Kelly Simpson
Rapid City, SD
Lots of sharp Cheddar
cheese makes this soup
rich, creamy and flavorful.

Toasty Ham & Swiss Stacks

2 T. mayonnaise
4 t. Dijon mustard
2 t. fresh dill, finely chopped
salt and pepper to taste
1 lb. sliced mushrooms
2 T. olive oil
8 slices rye bread, toasted
4 slices deli ham
4 slices Swiss cheese
4 thin slices red onion

In a small bowl, whisk together
mayonnaise, mustard, dill, salt
and pepper; set aside. In a skillet
over medium-high heat, sauté
mushrooms in oil, stirring
occasionally, for 5 minutes, or until
liquid evaporates; remove from heat.
Spread 4 toast slices with mayonnaise
mixture. Layer each slice with ham,
mushrooms, cheese and onion. Place
on an ungreased baking sheet. Broil
under a preheated broiler, about
4 inches from heat, for one to
2 minutes, until lightly golden and
cheese is melted. Top with remaining
toast slices. Makes 4 servings.

51

Kristan Vaughn
Gooseberry Patch

Filled with ham, Swiss
cheese and sautéed
mushrooms, these sandwiches
can also be served
open-faced.

Shoepeg & Green Bean Casserole

15-oz. can shoepeg corn, drained
14-1/2 oz. can green beans,
   drained
10-3/4 oz. can cream of celery soup
1 c. sour cream
1 c. shredded Cheddar cheese
1 c. round buttery crackers,
   crushed
1/2 c. butter, melted

Mix corn, green beans, soup, sour
cream and cheese together. Spread in
a greased 2-quart casserole dish. Top
with cracker crumbs; drizzle butter
over top. Bake, uncovered, at
350 degrees for one hour, or until
golden. Makes 6 to 8 servings.

Kathie McWherter
Bentonville, AR

A new spin on a traditional
side dish.

Chicken Corn Chowder Olé

3 T. butter
1-1/2 lbs. boneless, skinless
   chicken breast, cut into
   bite-size pieces
1/2 c. onion, chopped
1 to 2 cloves garlic, minced
2 cubes chicken bouillon
1 c. hot water
1/2 to 1 t. ground cumin
1 pt. half-and-half
8-oz. pkg. shredded Monterey
   jack cheese
16-oz. can creamed corn
4-oz. can chopped green chiles
1/4 to 1 t. hot pepper sauce
1 tomato, chopped

Melt butter in a Dutch oven over
medium heat; brown chicken, onion
and garlic until chicken is no longer
pink. Dissolve bouillon in hot water;
add to chicken mixture. Stir in
cumin; bring to a boil. Reduce heat;
cover and simmer for 5 minutes.
Add half-and-half, cheese, corn,
chiles and hot sauce. Cook and stir
over low heat until cheese is melted.
Stir in tomato; serve immediately.
Makes 6 to 8 servings.

53

Mary Gage
Wakewood, CA
An old favorite goes south
of the border for a spicy
new taste! Serve with
crispy tortilla chips.

Fluffy French Bread Stuffing

8 c. soft French bread, cubed
1 c. saltine crackers, crushed
1 t. dried sage
1 c. onion, chopped
1/2 c. celery, chopped
1/2 c. butter
10-3/4 oz. cream of chicken soup
2 eggs, beaten
1/4 c. fresh parsley, chopped

Combine bread cubes, cracker crumbs and sage in a large bowl; set aside. In a skillet over medium heat, cook onion and celery in butter until tender. Pour onion mixture over bread mixture. Add soup, eggs and parsley; toss lightly. Makes enough to stuff a 6 to 8-pound turkey or two, 3 to 4-pound chickens. Can also be placed in a lightly greased 4-quart casserole dish; cover with aluminum foil and bake at 350 degrees for one hour. Makes 8 servings.

Rachel Meinert
Shelby Township, MI
Our family can't get enough of this sage-flavored stuffing at Christmas...I usually have to make two batches!

Mack's Honey Apple Rings

1/2 c. honey
2 T. vinegar
1/4 t. cinnamon
1/4 t. salt
4 Golden Delicious apples, cored
   and cut into 1/2-inch rings

Combine honey, vinegar, cinnamon
and salt in a large skillet; bring to a
boil over medium heat. Add apple
rings to skillet. Reduce heat and
simmer for 8 to 10 minutes until
tender, turning apples once.
Makes 4 servings.

55

Vickie Roddie
Evergreen, CO

A scrumptious garnish for
pork chops or sausage.

Orange Chicken Italiano

4 boneless, skinless chicken breasts
1 c. orange juice
1/2 c. white wine or chicken broth
1/2 T. Italian seasoning
paprika to taste
1 onion, chopped
1 tomato, chopped
1/4 lb. sliced mushrooms
1 t. olive oil

Place chicken in a lightly greased shallow casserole dish. Combine orange juice and wine or broth; drizzle over chicken. Sprinkle with seasonings. Bake, uncovered, at 350 degrees for 30 minutes. While chicken bakes, sauté onion, tomato and mushrooms in oil until tender. Spoon vegetables over chicken; return to oven and bake, uncovered, for 30 additional minutes, or until chicken tests done. Serves 4.

Jennifer Eveland-Kupp
Blandon, PA
Serve over wild rice with fresh steamed vegetables for an effortless dinner.

Chicken Cacciatore

1 lb. boneless, skinless chicken
   breast, cubed
2 T. oil
28-oz. jar spaghetti sauce
14-1/2 oz. can diced tomatoes
1 green pepper, sliced
1 onion, chopped
2 cloves garlic, minced
1 t. Italian seasoning
salt and pepper to taste
cooked pasta or rice
Garnish: grated Parmesan cheese

In a large skillet over medium heat,
brown chicken in oil. Drain; stir in
remaining ingredients except cheese.
Reduce heat; cover and simmer until
vegetables are tender. Serve over
cooked pasta or rice, sprinkled with
cheese. Makes 2 to 4 servings.

Jenifer Minekheim
Garden Grove, CA
Try Italian-seasoned
diced tomatoes for even
more flavor.

57

Turkey & Wild Rice Casserole

6-oz. pkg. long-grain & wild rice,
   cooked
2 c. cooked turkey, diced
10-3/4 oz. can cream of
   mushroom soup
6-1/2 oz. can sliced mushrooms,
   drained
1 c. celery, thinly sliced
1 c. red pepper, chopped

Combine all ingredients in a large
bowl. Spread in a lightly greased
11"x7" baking pan. Bake, covered,
at 350 degrees for 30 to 40 minutes.
Serves 4 to 6.

Margaret Scoresby
Mosinee, WI
We have shared this tasty
recipe with many friends
over the years! It's
easy to double...great
for drop-in guests.

Shrimp Monterey

2 cloves garlic, minced
2 T. butter
2 lbs. uncooked medium shrimp, peeled and cleaned
1/2 c. white wine or chicken broth
2 c. shredded Monterey Jack cheese
2 T. fresh parsley, minced

In a skillet over medium heat, sauté garlic in butter for one minute. Add shrimp; cook for 4 to 5 minutes, or until pink. Using a slotted spoon, transfer shrimp to a greased 11"x7" baking pan; set aside and keep warm. Pour wine or broth into skillet; bring to a boil. Cook and stir for 5 minutes. Pour over shrimp; top with cheese and parsley. Bake, uncovered, at 350 degrees for 10 minutes, or until cheese is melted. Serves 4 to 6.

59

Donna Nowicki
Center City, MN

Garlic and shrimp...what a scrumptious combination! Serve over buttered spinach fettuccine.

Ham & Shrimp Risotto

2 T. butter
7-oz. pkg. chicken-flavored rice
    vermicelli mix, uncooked
2-3/4 c. water
2 c. cooked ham, diced
1 lb. cooked, peeled medium
    shrimp
1/4 c. celery, diced
1/4 c. green pepper, diced
1 T. dried, minced onion
1/4 t. hot pepper sauce
1/4 t. pepper

Melt butter in a large saucepan over
medium heat. Add uncooked rice
vermicelli mix and sauté just until
golden. Stir in remaining ingredients;
reduce heat, cover and simmer for
15 minutes. Serves 4 to 6.

Patricia Perkins
Shenandoah, IA

Add a little more hot
pepper sauce if you like
it extra spicy!

Apple-Glazed Pork Chops

4 pork loin chops
1/2 t. dried thyme
salt and pepper to taste
1 to 2 T. oil
1/2 c. apple jelly
1 T. Dijon mustard
1-1/2 T. butter

Sprinkle pork chops with thyme, salt and pepper. Heat oil in a large skillet over medium-high heat; sauté until golden and cooked through. Remove pork chops from skillet; set aside. Add jelly to skillet; cook until melted, scraping up any browned bits. Stir in mustard and butter; cook until bubbly and thickened. Return pork chops to skillet; turn to coat. Serve with sauce from skillet on the side. Makes 4 servings.

61

Diane Cohen
Kennesaw, GA
Delicious and oh-so simple to fix.

Bruschetta Chicken Bake

14-1/2 oz. can diced tomatoes with
    basil and onion
6-oz. pkg. herb-flavored stuffing
    mix
1/2 c. water
1-1/2 lbs. boneless, skinless
    chicken breasts, cubed
1 c. shredded mozzarella cheese

Combine tomatoes, stuffing mix and
water in a medium bowl. Stir just until
moistened; set aside. Arrange chicken
in a lightly greased 13"x9" baking
pan; sprinkle with cheese. Top with
stuffing mixture. Bake, uncovered,
at 400 degrees for 20 to 25 minutes,
or until chicken is cooked through.
Serves 6.

Renae Shingleton
Poca, WV

Add a crisp tossed salad
and a basket of hot garlic
bread...a festive dinner
is served!

Meatballs & Sauce

1 lb. ground beef
1 c. bread crumbs
2 eggs, beaten
1/2 c. grated Parmesan cheese
3 T. fresh Italian parsley,
  chopped
1. T. garlic powder
1 t. salt
1 t. pepper
2 to 4 T. olive oil
2 28-oz. cans crushed tomatoes
dried basil to taste
cooked spaghetti or hard rolls

63

In a large bowl, mix ground beef, bread crumbs, eggs, Parmesan cheese and seasonings. Form into 2-inch balls. In a large skillet over medium-high heat, fry meatballs in oil. Brown on all sides. Place meatballs in a large pot; add tomatoes. Simmer over low heat for at least an hour, stirring frequently. Add basil as desired. Serve meatballs and sauce over cooked spaghetti, or spoon into hard rolls to serve as sandwiches. Serves 4.

Patty Matteo
Colorado Springs, CO
Mom always made meatballs & sauce just about every Sunday, and I made it for my two boys too...now my grandchildren love it!

Steak & Spinach Pinwheels

1-1/4 lbs. beef flank steak or top
    round steak, halved lengthwise
3/4 t. lemon-pepper seasoning
1/4 t. salt
8 slices bacon, partially cooked
10-oz. pkg. frozen chopped
    spinach, thawed, drained
    and pressed dry
2 T. dry bread crumbs
1/2 t. dried thyme

With a sharp knife, score both pieces of steak in a diamond pattern with cuts one-inch apart. Repeat on other side. Place one piece of steak between 2 lengths of wax paper; pound lightly into a 10-inch by 6-inch rectangle. Repeat with second piece. Blend seasoning and salt; sprinkle each steak evenly with half of mixture. Arrange 4 slices of bacon lengthwise on each. Combine remaining ingredients in a bowl; spread half of spinach mixture over each steak. Starting at a short end, roll up each steak. Place seam-side down on an aluminum foil-lined, lightly greased broiler pan. Broil for 11 to 13 minutes, to desired doneness. Let stand for 2 to 3 minutes before slicing. Serves 6.

Amy Nicol
Marysville, OH
Such a pretty presentation
for special occasions.

Hearty Ham Alfredo Bake

16-oz. pkg. homestyle wide
  egg noodles
1/4 c. butter, sliced
2 16-oz. jars Alfredo sauce
1 to 2 c. milk
8-oz. pkg. shredded Swiss cheese
2 c. cooked ham, cubed
1/2 c. grated Parmesan cheese,
  divided
salt and pepper to taste

Cook noodles as package directs; drain. Toss hot noodles with butter and set aside. In a microwave-safe bowl, stir together sauce and milk to desired consistency. Microwave on high for about 5 minutes. Spray a 4-1/2 quart casserole dish with non-stick vegetable spray. Ladle one cup of sauce mixture into dish; add 1/3 each of noodles, Swiss cheese and ham cubes. Sprinkle with 1/4 cup Parmesan cheese. Repeat layering. Add salt and pepper to taste. Cover and bake at 350 degrees for 35 to 40 minutes. Makes 6 to 8 servings.

Dale Parker
Swartz Creek, MI
Our family enjoys this easy, delicious dish any time of the year. Serve with steamed broccoli.

Nutty Sausage & Cranberry Stuffing

16-oz. pkg. cornbread stuffing mix
2 c. chicken broth
1 egg, beaten
1/2 c. butter, divided
1 c. onion, chopped
1 c. celery, chopped
1 c. ground Italian pork sausage,
  browned and drained
1 c. sweetened dried cranberries
1/2 c. chopped pecans

Prepare stuffing mix according to package directions, using broth, egg and 1/4 cup butter; set aside. Sauté onion and celery in remaining butter until translucent. Stir onion mixture and remaining ingredients into stuffing; toss well to coat. Spread in a lightly greased 13"x9" baking pan. Cover and bake at 350 degrees for 30 minutes. Serves 8 to 10.

Layna Jarrett
Pennsboro, WV

Whether you call it stuffing or dressing, we think this recipe is scrumptious.

Raspberry-Orange Turkey Breast

3-lb. boneless turkey breast
1 c. orange juice
1 t. orange zest
1 t. dried sage
1/2 t. dried thyme
salt to taste
1/2 t. pepper
1-1/2 c. frozen raspberries
1/3 c. sugar

Place turkey breast in a lightly greased 9"x9" baking pan. Drizzle with orange juice; sprinkle with orange zest, sage, thyme, salt and pepper. Bake, uncovered, at 350 degrees for 1-1/2 hours, basting occasionally with pan juices. Near the end of baking time, toss together raspberries and sugar; spoon around turkey breast and return to oven for final 15 minutes. Let stand for 10 minutes before slicing. Serve spoonfuls of berries over slices. Serves 6.

67

Liz Plotnick-Snay
Gooseberry Patch

This sweet & savory turkey is always a hit at our house!

Tangy Chicken Piccata

1 lb. boneless, skinless chicken
   breasts
2 T. all-purpose flour
1 T. oil
1/2 c. orange juice
1/4 c. honey mustard
1/4 c. orange marmalade
1/4 t. dried rosemary, crushed
1 orange, peeled, quartered and
   thinly sliced

Dredge chicken in flour; set aside. Heat oil in a large skillet over medium heat. Add chicken and cook for 5 minutes, or until golden on both sides. Add juice, mustard, marmalade and rosemary; bring to a boil. Reduce heat; simmer for 5 minutes, or until chicken juices run clear. Stir in orange slices and heat through. Serves 4.

Barb Bargdill
Gooseberry Patch

A family favorite that's worthy of a holiday meal! Serve with a spinach salad and a savory rice pilaf.

Chicken & Mushroom Bake

16-oz. pkg. medium egg noodles, cooked
8-oz. can sliced water chestnuts, drained
2 10-3/4 oz. cans cream of mushroom soup
1 onion, chopped
3 c. shredded Cheddar cheese
2-oz. jar chopped pimentos, drained
1-1/2 c. chicken broth
1 c. milk
1 t. salt
pepper to taste
6 boneless, skinless chicken breasts, cooked and cubed

Combine all ingredients except chicken in a large bowl. Mix well and fold in chicken. Pour into a greased 13"x9" baking pan; cover and refrigerate for 12 hours to overnight. Bake, covered, at 325 degrees for 60 to 70 minutes. Let stand for 15 minutes before cutting into squares to serve. Serves 6.

Nancy Molldrem
Eau Claire, WI
Here's a hearty casserole you can rely on...it always seems to hit the spot!

69

Fire & Spice Baked Ham

5-1/2 to 6-lb. fully-cooked
   ham half
1/2 c. red pepper jelly
1/2 c. pineapple preserves
1/4 c. brown sugar, packed
1/4 t. ground cloves

Trim off rind and excess fat from ham; score fat in a diamond pattern. Place ham on a broiler pan sprayed with non-stick vegetable spray. Combine remaining ingredients in a small saucepan over low heat, stirring with a whisk until well blended. Brush 1/3 of jelly mixture over ham. Bake, uncovered, at 425 degrees for 5 minutes. Turn down oven temperature to 325 degrees. Bake ham for an additional 45 minutes, basting with remaining jelly mixture every 15 minutes. Transfer ham to a serving platter; let stand for 15 minutes before slicing. Makes 8 to 10 servings.

Linda Belon
Steubenville, OH
Is there anything more taste-tempting than the aroma of a baked ham? We don't think so!

Shrimp Creole

2 to 4 T. oil
2 onions, chopped
1 c. celery, chopped
1 green pepper, sliced
8-oz. can tomato sauce
14-1/2 oz. can diced tomatoes
10-oz. can diced tomatoes
   with chiles
1/2 c. water
1 bay leaf
2 t. sugar
2 t. salt
4 lbs. uncooked large shrimp,
   cleaned and peeled
cooked rice

71

Heat oil in a large skillet over medium heat. Add onions, celery and green pepper; cook slowly until tender. Add remaining ingredients except shrimp and rice; reduce heat and simmer for 45 minutes. Bring a large kettle of salted water to a boil over high heat. Drop shrimp into boiling water. Simmer for 5 minutes; drain. Add shrimp to tomato mixture in skillet and heat through. Discard bay leaf before serving. Serve over cooked rice. Makes 8 to 10 servings.

Robin Glass
Hewitt, TX
My grandma used to make this dish whenever we came to visit her. I still make it often...it sure brings back memories!

Chicken-Sausage Étouffée

**Robin Dusenbery
San Antonio, TX**

A tried & true old family recipe...it always takes me right back to our days in southern Louisiana.

1 T. olive oil
1 onion, chopped
1 green pepper, chopped
2 to 3 stalks celery, chopped
1 lb. boneless, skinless chicken breast, cut into 1-inch cubes
1 lb. smoked pork sausage, sliced into bite-size pieces
10-oz. can diced tomatoes with chiles
10-oz. can spicy diced tomatoes with chiles
2 10-3/4 oz. cans cream of mushroom soup
6-oz. can tomato paste
cooked rice

In a Dutch oven over medium heat, place oil, onion, green pepper, celery and chicken. Cook until chicken juices run clear, stirring occasionally. Place sausage in a microwave-safe dish with just enough water to cover. Microwave on high for 5 minutes. Drain sausage and add to ingredients in Dutch oven. Add both cans of tomatoes; reduce heat to low and simmer for 10 minutes. Stir in soup and tomato paste; stir until well blended. Simmer until bubbly. Serve over hot cooked rice. Serves 4 to 6.

Roasted Citrus-Herb Salmon

1 T. fresh parsley, chopped
1 T. fresh thyme, chopped
1 T. garlic, minced
1 T. olive oil
2 t. lemon zest
2 t. lime zest
1-1/2 t. salt
1/2 t. pepper
2 to 3-lb. salmon fillet

Combine all ingredients except salmon in a small bowl; set aside. Arrange salmon on a parchment paper-lined baking sheet; spread herb mixture over salmon. Bake, uncovered, at 400 degrees for 12 to 15 minutes, or until salmon flakes easily with a fork. Serves 4 to 6.

73

Karen Ensign
Providence, UT

With so many Christmas goodies on hand, we always welcome this delicious, light-tasting main dish.

Gran's Rosemary Roast Chicken

4-lb. roasting chicken
1 t. salt
1/4 t. pepper
1 onion, quartered
8 cloves garlic, pressed
1/4 c. fresh rosemary, chopped
1/4 c. butter, melted

Place chicken in a greased large roasting pan; sprinkle with salt and pepper. Place onion, garlic and rosemary inside chicken; brush butter over chicken. Bake, uncovered, at 400 degrees for 1-1/2 hours, basting occasionally with pan juices, until golden and juices run clear when pierced. Let stand for several minutes before carving. Serves 4 to 6.

Audrey Lett
Newark, DE

Tuck some tiny new potatoes and baby carrots around the chicken for a complete meal...so festive and delicious!

Hometown Chicken Pot Pie

3 to 4 lbs. boneless, skinless
    chicken breasts, cooked
    and cubed
2 16-oz. pkgs. frozen mixed
    vegetables, thawed
10-3/4 oz. can cream of chicken
    soup
10-3/4 oz. can cream of celery
    soup
1/2 c. chicken broth
1 c. biscuit baking mix
1/2 c. milk
1/2 c. margarine, melted
salt and pepper to taste

Arrange chicken in an ungreased
deep 13"x9" baking pan; set aside.
Mix vegetables with soups and broth;
pour over chicken. Combine biscuit
mix, milk and margarine; spread over
filling. Add salt and pepper to taste.
Bake, uncovered, at 375 degrees for
one hour, until bubbly and golden.
Serves 6.

75

Kim Williams
West Columbia, SC

The crust on this pie
is spooned over the
filling rather than being
rolled out...so easy!

German-Style Short Ribs

3 lbs. beef short ribs
2 T. oil
10-1/2 oz. can French onion soup
1 c. water
1 T. lemon juice
1/4 t. ground cloves
1/4 t. pepper
2 to 3 slices pumpernickel bread,
    crumbled
cooked egg noodles

In a large soup pot over medium heat,
brown ribs in oil for 6 to 8 minutes;
drain. Add remaining ingredients
except bread and noodles; bring to a
boil. Reduce heat to low; simmer for
1-1/2 to 2 hours, stirring occasionally.
Stir in bread and serve over noodles.
Serves 4.

Lynn Cisco
Princeville, IL
On chilly winter evenings,
the kitchen smells so warm
and inviting when this is
simmering on the stove.

Penne with Sausage & Cheese

1 lb. hot or mild Italian ground
   pork sausage
3 cloves garlic, chopped
26-oz. jar marinara sauce with
   cabernet and herbs
1/2 t. red pepper flakes
1/2 t. salt
1/2 t. pepper
1 c. shredded mozzarella cheese
12-oz. pkg. penne pasta, cooked
Garnish: grated Parmesan
   cheese, chopped fresh parsley

77

In a skillet over medium heat, cook
sausage until browned; drain. Add
garlic and cook until tender, about
2 minutes. Stir in sauce and
seasonings. Stir sauce mixture into
cooked pasta; transfer mixture to a
greased 12"x8" baking pan. Top with
mozzarella cheese. Bake, covered, at
375 degrees for 25 to 30 minutes,
until bubbly and cheese has melted.
Remove from oven; sprinkle with
Parmesan cheese and parsley. Makes
6 servings.

Bev Bornheimer
Lyons, NY
Everybody loves this
hearty, cheesy casserole!
It's just right for holiday
carry-ins or even for your
family dinner on Christmas.

Herbed Roast Turkey

Carolen Collins
Kansas City, MO

You'll find this turkey is tender, moist and flavorful. Serve the remaining herb butter with warm dinner rolls.

12 to 14-lb. turkey
6 T. Herb Butter, softened and
   divided
1 T. salt
1 t. pepper
1 onion, quartered
4 stalks celery, chopped
1 lemon, quartered

Rinse turkey and pat dry; place in a roasting pan. Gently loosen skin on breast; spread one tablespoon butter under skin. Rub turkey inside and out with remaining butter; sprinkle with salt and pepper. Place onion, celery and lemon inside turkey. Insert a meat thermometer into thickest part of thigh; cover loosely with aluminum foil. Roast at 325 degrees for 2-1/2 hours; uncover. Roast for an additional hour, basting with drippings every 20 minutes, until thermometer reads 180 degrees. Transfer turkey to a platter; cover. Let rest for 20 minutes and carve. Serves 12 to 14.

Herb Butter:

1 lb. butter, softened
4 t. lemon juice
1/2 t. garlic powder
1 t. each dried oregano, chives,
   thyme, rosemary, tarragon,
   finely crushed

Blend well; form into a log. Wrap with plastic wrap; chill overnight.

Turkey Tetrazzini

8-oz. pkg. thin spaghetti,
  uncooked
2 cubes chicken bouillon
2 to 3 T. dried, minced onion
2 10-3/4 oz. cans cream of
  mushroom soup
8-oz. container sour cream
1/2 c. milk
salt and pepper to taste
2 c. cooked turkey, cubed
8-oz. can sliced mushrooms,
  drained
Optional: 1 c. frozen peas,
  thawed
8-oz. pkg. shredded Cheddar
  cheese

Cook spaghetti according to package
directions, adding bouillon and
onion to cooking water. Drain and
place in a large bowl. Stir together
soup, sour cream, milk, salt and
pepper in a medium bowl. Fold in
turkey, mushrooms and peas, if using.
Lightly stir mixture into spaghetti,
coating well. Pour into a lightly
greased 13"x9" baking pan; top with
cheese. Bake, covered, at 350 degrees
for 30 to 40 minutes, until hot and
bubbly. Makes 6 servings.

Jennie Gist
Gooseberry Patch

This yummy casserole is
our family's favorite way
to enjoy leftover holiday
turkey. It's easy to toss
together, too.

79

Balsamic Chicken & Pears

2 t. oil, divided
4 boneless, skinless chicken breasts
2 Bosc pears, cored and cut into
   8 wedges
1 c. chicken broth
3 T. balsamic vinegar
2 t. cornstarch
1-1/2 t. sugar
1/4 c. dried cherries or raisins

Heat one teaspoon oil in a large skillet over medium-high heat; add chicken. Cook until golden and cooked through, about 5 minutes per side. Transfer to a plate; keep warm. Heat remaining oil in same skillet; add pears and cook until tender and golden. In a small bowl, combine broth, vinegar, cornstarch and sugar. Stir broth mixture into skillet with pears; add cherries or raisins. Bring to a boil over medium heat; cook for one minute, stirring constantly. Return chicken to skillet; heat through, spooning sauce over chicken. Serves 4.

Shirl Parsons
Cape Carteret, NC
The flavors in this dish blend together so well... very, very tasty!

Lasagna Florentine

1 lb. ground beef
1/2 c. onion, chopped
2 to 3 cloves garlic, minced
26-oz. jar spaghetti sauce,
    divided
16-oz. container cottage cheese
10-oz. pkg. frozen spinach,
    thawed and drained
12-oz. pkg. shredded mozzarella
    cheese, divided
1/2 c. grated Parmesan cheese,
    divided
2 eggs, beaten
9 lasagna noodles, cooked

Brown ground beef, onion and garlic. Drain; stir in spaghetti sauce and set aside. In a large bowl, combine cottage cheese, spinach, 2 cups mozzarella cheese, 1/4 cup Parmesan cheese and eggs. In an ungreased 13"x9" baking pan, layer one cup sauce mixture, 3 noodles and 1/2 cup cottage cheese mixture; repeat layering once. Top with remaining 3 noodles, sauce mixture, mozzarella and Parmesan. Cover with aluminum foil; bake at 350 degrees for 30 minutes. Uncover; bake for an additional 15 minutes. Let stand for 10 minutes before serving. Makes 9 servings.

Diane Cohen
Kennesaw, GA

Extra-special lasagna for the holiday...all dressed up with three kinds of cheese!

Graham Pralines

1 sleeve graham crackers
1/2 c. butter
1/2 c. margarine
1 c. brown sugar, packed
1/8 t. salt
1 c. chopped pecans

Cover a baking sheet with aluminum foil; spray lightly with non-stick vegetable spray. Break crackers and arrange on baking sheet; set aside. Melt butter, margarine, sugar and salt together in a saucepan over low heat. Bring to a boil and boil for 2 minutes; pour over crackers. Sprinkle pecans over top; bake at 350 degrees for 10 to 12 minutes. Let cool; break apart. Makes about 2 dozen.

Sandi Boothman
Camden, MI
A friend gave me this easy recipe...it's wonderful for the holidays. Try cinnamon grahams too...yum!

Candy Cane Thumbprints

2/3 c. butter, softened
1/2 c. sugar
1/4 t. salt
1 egg, beaten
1 t. vanilla extract
1-1/2 c. all-purpose flour
Garnish: finely crushed
   peppermint candies

With an electric mixer on low speed, blend butter, sugar and salt. Mix in egg and vanilla. Beat in as much flour as possible; stir in remaining flour. Cover; chill for one hour. Shape dough into one-inch balls; place 2 inches apart on ungreased baking sheets. Bake at 375 degrees for 8 to 10 minutes, until lightly golden around edges. Remove from oven; make a thumbprint in each cookie with thumb. Cool. Pipe filling into centers; sprinkle with crushed candy. Makes about 3 dozen.

Filling:

1/4 c. butter, softened
1/4 t. peppermint extract
1-1/2 c. powdered sugar
2 to 3 t. milk

Blend butter and extract. Gradually add powdered sugar and milk to a piping consistency.

83

Jennifer Martineau
Gooseberry Patch

My little daughter insists on making the thumbprints herself...won't Santa love finding a plate of these cookies on Christmas Eve!

Peanut Butter Fudge

Leigh Ann Oravecz
Pittsburgh, PA
Cut into shapes with a mini cookie cutter...stack, wrap in cello and tie with a ribbon for fun!

2-1/2 c. sugar
1/4 c. butter
5-oz. can evaporated milk
3/4 t. salt
1 c. creamy peanut butter
7-oz. jar marshmallow creme
1 c. peanut butter chips
1 t. vanilla extract
Optional: 1/2 c. chopped nuts

Line a 9"x9" baking pan with aluminum foil; butter lightly and set aside. Combine sugar, butter, evaporated milk and salt in a large heavy saucepan. Cook over medium heat until sugar dissolves, stirring occasionally; bring to a full rolling boil. Reduce heat slightly. Boil, stirring constantly, for 5 minutes. Remove from heat. Add peanut butter, marshmallow creme, peanut butter chips and vanilla; beat until well mixed. Stir in nuts, if using. Spread in prepared pan; chill for 2 to 3 hours, until firm. Lift fudge from pan; peel off foil and cut into squares. Makes about 2-1/2 pounds.

Chocolate Variation:

To make chocolate fudge, use 2 cups semi-sweet chocolate chips instead of the peanut butter chips and the peanut butter.

Raspberry-Marshmallow Cookie Pizza

18-oz. tube refrigerated sugar
  cookie dough
7-oz. jar marshmallow creme
12-oz. jar red raspberry jam
1 c. milk chocolate chips

Spray a 12" pizza pan with non-stick
vegetable spray. Spread out dough
evenly in the pan, using your fingers
to flatten. Pinch up dough to form
a rim around the edges. Bake at
350 degrees for 12 to 18 minutes,
until golden. Let cool completely
on pan. Spread marshmallow creme
evenly over cooled cookie to within
1/2-inch of edge. Spread jam over
marshmallow creme; set aside. Place
chocolate chips in a microwave-safe
bowl. Microwave on high for one
minute; stir. Microwave an additional
10 to 20 seconds, stirring until
smooth and melted. Drizzle melted
chocolate over cookie. Chill for at
least one hour. Cut into thin wedges.
Makes 20 to 24 servings.

Tessa Floehr
Marysville, OH

A scrumptious dessert
pizza...fancy enough to
serve at a holiday tea,
yet simple enough for
kids' parties too.

Michelle's Caramel Corn

12 c. popped popcorn
1 c. dark brown sugar, packed
1/2 c. light corn syrup
1/3 c. butter
1 T. light molasses
1-1/2 t. vanilla extract
1/2 t. baking soda
1/2 t. salt

Spray a large roaster pan with non-stick vegetable spray. Place popcorn in pan and set aside. Combine brown sugar, corn syrup, butter and molasses in a medium saucepan; bring to a boil over medium heat. Cook for 5 minutes, stirring once. Remove from heat; stir in vanilla, baking soda and salt. Pour hot mixture over popcorn, stirring to coat. Bake at 250 degrees for one hour, stirring every 15 minutes. Remove from oven; stir to break up. Cool for 15 minutes. Store in an airtight container for up to one week. Makes about 12 cups.

Michelle Sheridan
Gooseberry Patch

Oh-so light, sweet and crunchy...yum! Tuck some into your favorite football fan's stocking for snacking during the big game.

Sugar Cookie Mittens

2 c. butter, softened
1-1/3 c. sugar
2 eggs, beaten
2 t. vanilla extract
5 c. all-purpose flour

Blend butter and sugar together; stir in eggs and vanilla. Add flour; mix until well blended. Shape into a ball; cover and chill for 4 hours to overnight. Roll out dough 1/4-inch thick on a lightly floured surface; cut out with cookie cutters as desired. Arrange cookies on lightly greased baking sheets. Bake at 350 degrees for 8 to 10 minutes, until golden. Frost cookies when cool. Makes 4 dozen.

87

Frosting:

4-1/2 c. powdered sugar
6 T. butter, melted
6 T. milk
2 T. vanilla extract
1 T. lemon juice
Optional: few drops food
    coloring

Combine all ingredients in a medium bowl. Beat with an electric mixer on low speed until smooth.

Tina Knotts
Cable, OH

Everybody needs a dependable cut-out cookie recipe for Christmas...this is mine! I collect cookie cutters and this works so well with them.

Walnut-Raisin Pie

3 eggs, beaten
2/3 c. sugar
1 c. corn syrup
1/3 c. butter, melted
1/2 t. cinnamon
1/2 t. nutmeg
1/2 t. ground cloves
1/2 t. salt
1 c. walnuts, coarsely chopped
2 c. raisins
9-inch pie crust

In a large bowl, beat together eggs, sugar, corn syrup, butter, spices and salt until well mixed. Stir in walnuts and raisins; pour into pie crust. Bake at 375 degrees for 40 to 50 minutes, until set. Cool before slicing. Serves 6 to 8.

Gloria Kaufmann
Orrville, OH

One of my husband's favorite pies! Have a cup of coffee or tea ready to enjoy with this rich pie.

Buckeyes

Vickie
Gooseberry Patch

Rich, peanut-buttery balls
dipped in chocolate...
they're irresistible at
the holidays or anytime!

16-oz. jar creamy peanut butter
1 c. butter, softened
6 c. powdered sugar
12-oz. pkg. semi-sweet
   chocolate chips
1/3 bar paraffin

Blend together peanut butter, butter
and powdered sugar, mixing with
hands. Shape into one-inch balls;
chill. Melt together chocolate chips
and paraffin over hot water in a
double boiler. Use a toothpick to
dip each ball in chocolate, leaving a
small spot uncovered. Arrange on
wax paper-lined baking sheet. With
the tip of a small knife, smooth over
hole left by toothpick. Place in cool
area or freezer to set. Makes about
5 to 6 dozen.

89

Ho-Ho Snowballs

Madison Oudemohl
Charleston, SC
Super-easy to make...and
they melt in your mouth!

2 6-oz. pkgs. white chocolate chips
1/4 c. heavy cream
2 T. bourbon or heavy cream
6-oz. pkg. slivered almonds, very
    finely ground
1-1/2 c. sweetened flaked coconut

Place chocolate chips and cream in
a medium bowl set over a pan of hot
(not boiling) water; stir until melted
and smooth. Stir in bourbon or cream
and almonds. Spread in a lightly
greased 8"x8" baking pan. Chill for
about one hour, until firm. Cut into
one-inch squares; roll each square into
a ball, then roll in coconut. Keep
chilled. Makes about 5 dozen.

Christmas Crunch

3 c. doughnut-shaped oat cereal
3 c. bite-size crispy corn cereal
squares
3 c. bite-size crispy rice cereal
squares
2 c. salted peanuts
12-oz. pkg. candy-coated
chocolates
1-1/2 lbs. white melting
chocolate disks

Combine all ingredients except
melting chocolate in a very large
bowl; set aside. Place chocolate in
a microwave-safe bowl. Microwave
on high for 2 to 3 minutes, stirring
every minute, until melted and
smooth. Pour melted chocolate over
cereal mixture; stir gently to coat.
Pour out onto wax paper; let harden.
Break into pieces; store in airtight
containers. Makes about 16 cups.

Julia Leone
Fairport, NY

This sweet mix looks oh-so
pretty in jars for gift-
giving. Just cover the lids
with fabric, then tie on a
ribbon and a tiny ornament.

Festive Holiday Gingerbread

12-oz. jar light molasses
1 c. butter, softened
3/4 c. dark brown sugar, packed
2 eggs, beaten
1 c. hot water
4 c. all-purpose flour
2 t. baking soda
1/2 t. salt
2-1/2 t. ground ginger
1/2 t. cinnamon
9-oz. pkg. condensed mincemeat,
    finely crumbled
Garnish: powdered sugar

In a large bowl, combine all ingredients
except mincemeat and powdered sugar.
Beat with an electric mixer on medium
speed for 2 to 3 minutes, until well
blended. Fold in mincemeat; spoon
into a greased Bundt® or tube pan.
Bake at 350 degrees for 45 to
50 minutes. Cool for 10 minutes.
Turn out onto a wire rack to cool
completely. Dust with powdered sugar.
Makes 10 to 12 servings.

Peggy Anderson
Easton, CT
When I lived in England, I
baked this delicious cake
for a charity cake stall at
a village fair...it won the
top bid of all!

GiGi's Cranberry Cobbler

3 c. biscuit baking mix
2 c. sugar
2 eggs, beaten
1/2 c. butter, softened
1 c. milk
3 c. cranberries

Mix baking mix, sugar, eggs and butter together; blend in milk. Stir in cranberries lightly, until evenly coated with batter. Pour into a greased and floured 13"x9" baking pan. Bake at 350 degrees for 50 to 55 minutes. Spoon Hot Butter Sauce over warm cobbler. Serves 8 to 10.

Hot Butter Sauce:

2 c. sugar
1 c. butter, sliced
2 c. whipping cream
2 t. vanilla extract

Combine ingredients in a deep medium saucepan over medium heat. Bring to a boil. Boil for about 5 minutes, stirring constantly.

93

Dawn Horton
Allen, TX
We all look forward to this cobbler each Christmas when my sweet mother-in-law makes it.

Peppermint Snowballs

1/2 c. peppermint candies, finely
   crushed and divided
1/4 c. plus 1/3 c. powdered sugar,
   divided
1 c. butter, softened
1 t. vanilla extract
2-1/4 c. all-purpose flour
1/4 t. salt

Combine 1/4 cup crushed candies and
1/4 cup powdered sugar; set aside. Beat
together butter, remaining powdered
sugar, remaining candies and vanilla
with an electric mixer on medium
speed. Stir in flour and salt. Shape into
one-inch balls; arrange one inch apart
on ungreased baking sheets. Bake at
325 degrees for 12 to 15 minutes, until
set but not brown. Immediately remove
from baking sheets; roll in reserved
candy mixture. Let cool completely on
a wire rack; roll again in candy mixture.
Makes about 2-1/2 dozen.

April Jacobs
Loveland, CO

Christmas classics with a
hint of mint that makes
them extra special.

Gingerbread Houses

graham crackers
cardboard square
assorted candies, pretzels, small
    cookies, cereals

Attach graham crackers together to
form a small house, using Royal Icing
as cement. Use a little icing to attach
house to cardboard square. Decorate
house and base as you like, using
icing to attach candies, pretzels,
cookies and cereals. Make as many
houses as you wish!

Royal Icing:

1/2 c. pasteurized egg whites
1/2 t. cream of tartar
16-oz. pkg. powdered sugar
several drops food coloring

Combine egg whites, cream of tartar
and powdered sugar in a large bowl.
Beat for several minutes with an
electric mixer on high speed until
smooth. Divide into small bowls
and color as desired. Makes about
2-1/2 cups.

Creative Team
Gooseberry Patch

Our artists decorated these
little houses...but it's so
easy, you can do it too!

Christmas Crinkle Cookies

12-oz. pkg. semi-sweet chocolate
  chips, divided
1-1/2 c. all-purpose flour
1-1/2 t. baking powder
1/4 t. salt
1 c. sugar
6 T. butter, softened
1-1/2 t. vanilla extract
2 eggs
3/4 c. powdered sugar

Place one cup chocolate chips in a
microwave-safe bowl. Microwave on
high setting for one minute; stir.
Microwave at additional 10-second
intervals, stirring until smooth. Cool
to room temperature. Combine flour,
baking powder and salt in a small bowl;
set aside. Blend sugar, butter and
vanilla in a large bowl; beat in melted
chocolate. Add eggs one at a time,
stirring well after each. Gradually beat
in flour mixture; stir in remaining
chips. Chill just until firm. Shape into
1-1/2 inch balls; roll generously in
powdered sugar. Place on ungreased
baking sheets. Bake at 350 degrees
for 10 to 15 minutes, until sides are set
and centers are still slightly soft. Cool
on baking sheets 2 minutes; place on
wire racks to cool completely. Makes
4 to 5 dozen.

Rachael Hall
McDonald, PA
Chocolatey morsels with a
snowy coating of powdered
sugar...yummy!

Minty Candy Canes

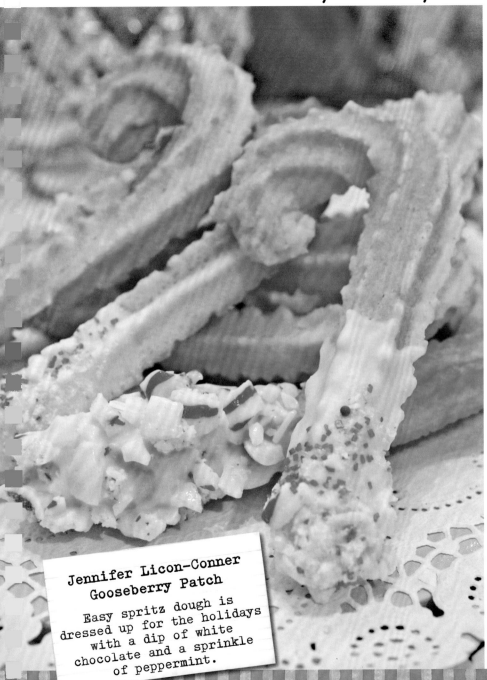

Jennifer Licon-Conner
Gooseberry Patch

Easy spritz dough is dressed up for the holidays with a dip of white chocolate and a sprinkle of peppermint.

3/4 c. butter, softened
1/2 c. sugar
1 t. baking powder
1 egg, beaten
1/2 t. peppermint extract
1-3/4 c. all-purpose flour
6 1-oz. sqs. white baking
   chocolate
1 T. shortening
1/3 c. peppermint candies,
   finely crushed

Beat together butter, sugar and baking powder with an electric mixer on medium speed. Add egg and extract; blend well. Beat in as much flour as possible with mixer; stir in any remaining flour. Pack dough into a cookie press fitted with a 1/2" star plate. Press out dough to form 4-inch-long sticks one inch apart on ungreased baking sheets; bend into candy-cane shape. Bake at 375 degrees for 7 to 9 minutes, or until edges are firm but not brown. Let cool on a wire rack. Melt white chocolate and shortening in a small heavy saucepan over low heat, stirring frequently. Dip the end of each cane into chocolate, letting excess drip off. Place on wax paper; sprinkle with crushed candies. Let harden. Makes 5 dozen.

Mee-Mee's Berry Gelatin

3.4-oz. pkg. raspberry gelatin mix
3.4-oz. pkg. lemon gelatin mix
2 c. boiling water
10-oz. pkg. frozen raspberries,
    thawed
1 c. whole-berry cranberry sauce
8-oz. can crushed pineapple,
    drained
1 c. lemon-lime soda

In a medium bowl, dissolve gelatin mixes in boiling water; stir well. Add raspberries and cranberry sauce; mix well. Stir in pineapple. Let cool briefly. Add soda; pour into a 9"x9" serving dish and refrigerate until set. Spread Vanilla Topping over gelatin; cut into squares. Serves 6 to 9.

Vanilla Topping:

1/4 c. instant vanilla pudding mix
1 c. milk
2 c. frozen whipped topping,
    thawed

Whisk together pudding mix and milk for 2 minutes; fold in topping.

Brooke Steinke
Williams, CA

My great-grandmother first made this gelatin recipe and now it wouldn't be Christmas without it!

Easiest-Ever Sugar Cookies

Virginia Watson
Scranton, PA

So easy to mix up, even
the kids can help...and of
course, they will want to!

3.4-oz. pkg. instant vanilla
   pudding mix
1/2 c. sugar
1/2 c. butter, softened
1 egg, beaten
1-1/2 c. all-purpose flour
1 t. baking powder
Optional: frosting, decorator
   sugar, candy sprinkles

Blend together pudding mix, sugar
and butter; stir in egg and set aside.
Mix flour and baking powder; blend
thoroughly into pudding mixture.
Chill dough until firm. Roll out
1/8-inch to 1/4-inch thick on a
lightly floured surface; cut with
desired cookie cutters. Place on
lightly greased baking sheets. Bake
at 350 degrees for 8 to 9 minutes.
When cool, frost and decorate, if
desired. Makes 2 to 3 dozen.

Powdered Sugar Frosting:

3 c. powdered sugar
2 to 3 T. milk
1 t. vanilla extract
few drops food coloring

Combine all ingredients in a large
bowl. Divide icing into small bowls.
Tint portions with food coloring
as desired.

Dipped Gingerbread Stars

1 c. shortening
1 c. brown sugar, packed
3/4 c. molasses
3/4 c. buttermilk
2 eggs, beaten
4-1/2 c. all-purpose flour
1 T. ground ginger
2 t. baking soda
1 t. salt
Garnish: white and semi-sweet
  chocolate chips, melted

Blend shortening and brown sugar together; add molasses, buttermilk and eggs. Blend well; set aside. In a separate bowl, mix flour, ginger, baking soda and salt; blend into shortening mixture. Mix well; refrigerate overnight. Roll out dough 1/4-inch thick on a lightly floured surface; cut out with a star cookie cutter. Arrange on ungreased baking sheets; bake at 400 degrees for 10 to 12 minutes. Let cool completely; dip half of each cookie into melted chocolate. Place on wax paper to set. Makes about 5 dozen.

Judee DeVine
Venetia, PA

Spicy and sweet with a jacket of chocolate, they're irresistible.

Cranberry Crumb Bars

1-1/2 c. plus 1/3 c. all-purpose
  flour, divided
1/3 c. powdered sugar
1 c. chilled butter, divided
8-oz. pkg. cream cheese,
  softened
14-oz. can sweetened
  condensed milk
1/4 c. lemon juice
2 T. cornstarch
3 T. brown sugar, packed and
  divided
16-oz. can whole-berry
  cranberry sauce
3/4 c. chopped walnuts

101

Combine 1-1/2 cups flour and powdered sugar; cut in 3/4 cup butter until crumbly. Press into a greased 13"x9" baking pan. Bake at 350 degrees for 15 to 20 minutes; cool. Beat cream cheese, condensed milk and lemon juice; spread over baked crust. Combine cornstarch and one tablespoon brown sugar; stir in cranberry sauce. Spread over cream cheese layer and set aside. Combine remaining brown sugar, flour, butter and nuts; sprinkle over filling. Bake at 325 degrees for 40 to 45 minutes, until golden. Cool in pan on a wire rack; chill for 3 hours before slicing. Makes one dozen.

Jo Ann
Gooseberry Patch

We can't wait 'til Christmas for these sweet-tart bar cookies... they've become a tradition!

Whipped Pumpkin Pie

15-oz. can pumpkin
2 10-oz. pkgs. mini marshmallows
1 t. cinnamon
12-oz. container frozen non-dairy
    whipped topping, thawed
2 9-inch graham cracker crusts
Optional: additional whipped
    topping

Combine pumpkin, marshmallows and cinnamon in a heavy saucepan. Stir over low heat until marshmallows are melted. Remove from heat; cover and let stand until mixture reaches room temperature. Fold in whipped topping. Divide evenly into pie crusts; chill for one hour before serving. If desired, garnish with dollops of whipped topping. Makes 2 pies; each serves 6 to 8.

Sarina Skidmore
Buffalo, MT
I created this recipe for my son, who is allergic to dairy products...now we all love it!

Gumdrop Cookies

1 c. butter, softened
1/2 c. sugar
1/2 c. brown sugar, packed
2 T. milk
1 t. vanilla extract
2-1/2 c. all-purpose flour
1 t. baking powder
3/4 c. gumdrops, chopped

Blend together butter and sugars. Beat in milk and vanilla; set aside. Stir together flour and baking powder; blend into butter mixture. Stir in gumdrops. Shape dough into two, 14-inch rolls. Wrap in plastic wrap; chill thoroughly. Cut into 1/4-inch slices; arrange on ungreased baking sheets. Bake at 375 degrees for 10 minutes. Makes about 4 to 5 dozen.

103

Linda Mills
Pasadena, MD
They look like they've been sprinkled with confetti... how fun! To cut the sticky gumdrops, dip kitchen shears in flour and snip away.

Mom's Italian Biscotti

5-1/2 c. all-purpose flour
1 T. plus 2 t. baking powder
3/4 c. butter, softened
1-1/2 c. sugar
6 eggs, beaten
zest and juice of 2 lemons
3-1/2 c. powdered sugar
Garnish: white candy sprinkles

Mix together flour, baking powder, butter and sugar; form a well in the center. Add eggs and lemon zest; knead until dough is smooth. Form dough into 2-inch balls. Roll each ball on a floured surface into a 7-inch rope. Twist ropes into knots; place on lightly greased baking sheets. Bake at 350 degrees for 15 to 18 minutes. Cool on a wire rack. Combine lemon juice and powdered sugar; drizzle over cookies. Add sprinkles, if desired. Makes 3 dozen.

Jeanette Toscano
Pomona, NY

My parents emigrated from Italy in the 1960's, bringing this recipe with them.

Cherry-Pecan Bread Pudding

2-lb. loaf French bread or
   homestyle white bread, cubed
4 c. milk
2 c. half-and-half
3/4 c. plus 2 T. sugar, divided
6 eggs, beaten
2 t. vanilla extract
1/2 t. cinnamon
1/2 c. dried tart cherries
1/2 c. chopped pecans
1/2 c. butter, melted

Spread bread cubes on a baking sheet; let dry overnight. In a saucepan over low heat, combine milk, half-and-half and 7 tablespoons sugar. Heat to 120 degrees on a candy thermometer; remove from heat. In a large bowl, combine eggs, vanilla, cinnamon and remaining sugar; blend with a whisk. Stir in cherries and pecans. Slowly whisk half of milk mixture into egg mixture; add remaining milk mixture. Stir in bread cubes; toss to mix and let stand for 5 minutes. Mix in melted butter; transfer mixture to a lightly greased 13"x10" baking pan. Bake at 350 degrees for 35 minutes, or until center is firm. Serve warm. Makes 8 to 10 servings.

105

Sharon Demers
Dolores, CO

My husband loves bread pudding! I've tried recipe after recipe until I came up with this one...we think it's perfect!

Strawberry Delight Cookies

1/4 c. butter, softened
8-oz. pkg. cream cheese, softened
1 egg, beaten
1/4 t. vanilla extract
18-1/2 oz. pkg. strawberry cake mix
1 c. canned strawberry frosting

Blend together butter and cream
cheese; stir in egg and vanilla. Add
dry cake mix 1/3 at a time, mixing well
after each addition. Cover and chill
for 30 minutes. Drop by teaspoonfuls
onto ungreased baking sheets. Bake at
375 degrees for 10 to 12 minutes. Place
frosting in a microwave-safe bowl.
Microwave for 15 to 30 seconds; drizzle
over cooled cookies. Makes 4 dozen.

Nola Coons
Gooseberry Patch

The secret is the cake
mix...it makes these
cookies so easy to whip up!

Lemon Icebox Cookies

Dani Strickland
Tallahassee, FL
Light and crisp, these
cookies are just right
with a cup of tea.

3/4 c. sugar, divided
3/4 c. brown sugar, packed
1 c. butter, softened
1-1/2 t. vanilla extract
1 egg, beaten
1 egg, separated
3 c. all-purpose flour
1-1/2 t. baking powder
3/4 t. salt
2 T. lemon juice
1 T. lemon zest
3/4 c. finely chopped nuts
Optional: lemon frosting

107

Combine 1/2 cup sugar, brown sugar,
butter, vanilla, egg and egg yolk;
blend well. Add flour, baking
powder, salt, lemon juice and zest;
mix well. Shape dough into two,
1-1/2 inch thick rolls; wrap in wax
paper. Refrigerate for one hour, or
until firm. Combine nuts and
remaining sugar in a small bowl.
Slightly beat egg white. Brush dough
with egg white; roll in nut mixture,
pressing in nuts firmly. Slice dough
1/4-inch thick. Place slices one inch
apart on greased baking sheets. Bake
at 400 degrees for 5 to 7 minutes, or
until lightly golden. Immediately
remove to wire racks. Decorate with
frosting, if desired. Makes 7 dozen.

INDEX

INDEX

Our Story

Back in 1984, we were next-door neighbors raising our families in the little town of Delaware, Ohio. We were two moms with small children looking for a way to do what we loved and stay home with the kids too. We shared a love of home cooking and making memories with family & friends. After many a conversation over the backyard fence, **Gooseberry Patch** was born.

We put together the first catalog & cookbooks at our kitchen tables and packed boxes from the basement, enlisting the help of our loved ones wherever we could. From that little family, we've grown to include an amazing group of creative folks who love cooking, decorating and creating as much as we do.

Hard to believe it's been over 25 years since those kitchen-table days. Today we're best known for our homestyle, family-friendly cookbooks, now recognized as national bestsellers! We love hand-picking the recipes and are tickled to share our inspiration, ideas and more with you. One thing's for sure, we couldn't have done it without our friends all across the country. Whether you've been along for the ride from the beginning or are just discovering us, welcome to our family!

Vickie & Jo Ann

Visit us online:
www.gooseberrypatch.com
1·800·854·6673

U.S. to Canadian Recipe Equivalents

Volume Measurements

1/4 teaspoon	1 mL
1/2 teaspoon	2 mL
1 teaspoon	5 mL
1 tablespoon = 3 teaspoons	15 mL
2 tablespoons = 1 fluid ounce	30 mL
1/4 cup	60 mL
1/3 cup	75 mL
1/2 cup = 4 fluid ounces	125 mL
1 cup = 8 fluid ounces	250 mL
2 cups = 1 pint =16 fluid ounces	500 mL
4 cups = 1 quart	1 L

Weights

1 ounce	30 g
4 ounces	120 g
8 ounces	225 g
16 ounces = 1 pound	450 g

Oven Temperatures

300° F	150° C
325° F	160° C
350° F	180° C
375° F	190° C
400° F	200° C
450° F	230° C

Baking Pan Sizes

Square

8x8x2 inches	2 L = 20x20x5 cm
9x9x2 inches	2.5 L = 23x23x5 cm

Rectangular

13x9x2 inches	3.5 L = 33x23x5 cm

Loaf

9x5x3 inches	2 L = 23x13x7 cm

Round

8x1-1/2 inches	1.2 L = 20x4 cm
9x1-1/2 inches	1.5 L = 23x4 cm

Recipe Abbreviations

t. = teaspoon	ltr. = liter
T. = tablespoon	oz. = ounce
c. = cup	lb. = pound
pt. = pint	doz. = dozen
qt. = quart	pkg. = package
gal. = gallon	env. = envelope

Kitchen Measurements

A pinch = 1/8 tablespoon	1 fluid ounce = 2 tablespoons
3 teaspoons = 1 tablespoon	4 fluid ounces = 1/2 cup
2 tablespoons = 1/8 cup	8 fluid ounces = 1 cup
4 tablespoons = 1/4 cup	16 fluid ounces = 1 pint
8 tablespoons = 1/2 cup	32 fluid ounces = 1 quart
16 tablespoons = 1 cup	16 ounces net weight = 1 pound
2 cups = 1 pint	
4 cups = 1 quart	
4 quarts = 1 gallon	